A History of Super Science

Chicago, Illinois

Raintree

© 2006 Raintree
Published by Raintree,
an imprint of Capstone Global Library, LLC
Chicago, Illinois

Customer Service   888–363–4266

Visit our website at www.heinemannraintree.com

Printed and bound in the United States of America,
North Mankato, MN

14 13 12
10 9 8 7 6 5 4

**Library of Congress Cataloging-in-
Publication Data**
Solway, Andrew.
   A history of super science : atoms and elements /
Andrew Solway.
        p. cm. -- (Fusion)
   Includes bibliographical references and index.
   ISBN 1-4109-1920-X (lib. bdg.) -- ISBN 1-4109-
1951-X (pbk.)
   1.   Chemistry--Juvenile literature. 2.   Atoms--
Juvenile literature. 3.   Chemical elements--Juvenile
literature. 4.   Chemists--Juvenile literature. 5.
Discoveries in science--Juvenile literature.   I. Title. II.
Series: Fusion (Chicago, Ill.)
   QD35.S65 2005
   540--dc22
                                       2005014547

ISBN 13: 978-1-4109-1920-5 (library binding-
hardcover)
ISBN 13: 978-1-4109-1951-9 (pbk)

092012
006924

Acknowledgments
The author and publishers are grateful to the
following for permission to reproduce copyright
material: Corbis pp. 4–5 (Royalty-Free), 13 (lower left)
(Royalty-Free), 13 (lower right) (Royalty-Free), 13 (top
left) (Royalty-Free), 19 (Archivo Iconografico, S.A.);
Creatas p. 13 (top right); Science Photo Library pp.
6–7 (Dirk Wiersma), 16–17 (Sheila Terry), 20 (Andrew
Lambert Photography), 23 (Sheila Terry), 26 (CCI
Archives), 22–23 (US Department Of Energy), 24–25
(Sheila Terry); The Art Archive p. 14–15 (Metropolitan
Museum of Art New York/Joseph Martin); The
Bridgeman Art Library pp. 21 (The Royal Institution,
London, UK), 10–11 (Derby Museum and Art Gallery,
UK), 8–9 (Palazzo Vecchio (Palazzo della Signoria)
Florence, Italy).

Cover photograph of a scientist, reproduced with
permission of Comstock Images.

Illustrations by Seb Burnett.

The publishers would like to thank Nancy Harris
and Harold Pratt for their assistance in the
preparation of this book.

Every effort has been made to contact copyright
holders of any material reproduced in this book.
Any omissions will be rectified in subsequent
printings if notice is given to the publishers.

Disclaimer
All the Internet addresses (URLs) given in this book
were valid at the time of going to press. However,
due to the dynamic nature of the Internet, some
addresses may have changed, or sites may have
changed or ceased to exist since publication. While
the author and publishers regret any inconvenience
this may cause readers, no responsibility for any
such changes can be accepted by either the author
or the publishers.

Contents

Any words appearing in the text in bold, **like this**, are explained in the glossary. You can also look out for them in the word box at the bottom of each page.

Thick Glasses and Wild Hair?

Cartoon scientists usually have thick glasses and wild hair. They are brilliant. Yet they are scatterbrained when it comes to everyday life. Of course, real scientists are not like this. Or are they?

Chemists are scientists who are interested in **substances**. A substance is something that you can touch and see. Chemists look at how substances join together. They also look at how substances can be separated. Chemists have made some important discoveries in the past. They have also done some strange things.

Let's look at a few chemists. These chemists first found out about **atoms** and **elements**. Yet before we do, what are atoms and elements?

atom	tiny piece that makes up every kind of substance
element	substance made of only one kind of atom
substance	something that you can touch and see

◀ *Chemists use lots of glass test tubes and flasks. The cleanup is a nightmare!*

The Simplest Things

Everything around us is made of **atoms**. Atoms are the smallest parts of a **substance**. You could fit millions of atoms into the period at the end of this sentence. There are many different kinds of atoms.

An **element** is made of only one kind of atom. Elements are simple substances.

A few things in your house might be elements. The pans in your kitchen may be made of aluminium. Aluminium is an element. It is made of aluminium atoms and nothing else.

Most substances are not as simple as elements. They are made of more than one kind of atom.

Now that we know about atoms and elements, we can get back to those crazy chemists . . .

◀ *Gold is an element. It can be found in rocks—but only if you are very lucky!*

The First Chemists

The earliest chemists were called **alchemists**. They did lots of mixing and heating of **substances**. A substance is something that you can touch and see. Yet alchemists were really interested in two things. They wanted to know how to live forever. They also wanted to know how to make gold!

Alchemists made some useful discoveries. Arnold of Villanova was an alchemist. He lived in Italy a long time ago. He had some pretty crazy ideas. He thought people could live for hundreds of years. To do so, people had to rub themselves with spices. They also had to eat chickens that had been fed snakes and vinegar!

Another alchemist was the first person we know of to discover an **element**…

alchemist   person who tried to make gold from other substances

◀ *This is how an alchemist's workshop may have looked.*

IOÁNES
STRATENSIS
FLANDRVS
1570

Hennig Brand made a ▼
new substance. It glowed
in the dark. He called
it phosphorus.

A golden liquid

Hennig Brand was a German **alchemist**. Like most alchemists, he wanted to make gold. He tried making gold from other metals. Yet this didn't work. So, he decided to use another **substance**. He tried making gold from **urine**!

First, he collected buckets of urine. He left them to sit for days. Then, he heated the urine. Next, Brand heated the urine at a high temperature. Some of the urine **evaporated**. It turned into a gas. Brand collected this gas and cooled it down. The gas became a solid when it cooled down.

The solid was white instead of gold. It also glowed in the dark! Brand had discovered a new **element**. He called it phosphorus.

▼ Brand collected many buckets of urine. He thought he could use urine to make gold.

11

evaporate	turn from a liquid into a gas
urine	mixture of water and unwanted chemicals from your body

Earth, Fire, Air, and Water

Robert Boyle was an English **alchemist**. He lived about 400 years ago. He was rich, so he didn't try making gold. In one experiment, he thought he had turned gold into another metal!

Boyle liked experimenting. He had a **laboratory** in his house. He did thousands of different experiments in it.

At that time, most people thought there were just four **elements**. They thought that these elements were earth (soil), fire, air, and water. Yet Boyle wasn't so sure. His experiments made him think that this idea was wrong. Soon, other chemists started to agree with him. But if air, fire, earth, and water were not elements, what were?

Telltale alchemist

Most alchemists kept their experiments secret. They never told anyone about them. Yet Boyle told everyone exactly how he did his experiments. He also told everyone what happened. Modern scientists now work in the same way.

laboratory   place for doing experiments

People used to think that fire, water, air, and earth were elements.

Boiling Hot

Antoine-Laurent Lavoisier was a French chemist. He was the first to figure out the **elements.** He lived about 100 years after Robert Boyle.

Lavoisier loved experiments. In one experiment, he heated water until it **evaporated** and became a gas. He collected the gas and cooled it. The gas turned back into water again. He did this again and again for 101 days!

Lavoisier did this experiment many times for a reason. Some scientists believed that water could be heated and changed to soil. Lavoisier showed that this idea was wrong. He didn't make any soil. Yet you might think he was a bit crazy to spend 101 days boiling water!

This painting shows ▶
Lavoisier with his wife,
Marie Anne. She helped with
many of his experiments.

Real elements at last

Lavoisier learned lots of things from his own experiments. He also looked at experiments that other people had done. He used these experiments to figure out new ideas.

Joseph Priestley was an English scientist. He showed that air was not a single **substance**. Lavoisier discovered that air was not an **element**. It could be split into many elements. Lavoisier also showed that water was not an element. He split water into two elements. These elements were hydrogen and oxygen.

Laviosier said that elements could not be split or broken down any further. He made a list of 33 substances that he thought were elements. Some of the elements in his list turned out to be wrong. Still, chemists were at last starting to understand elements.

◀ *Lavoisier is making water in this experiment. He is combining hydrogen and oxygen.*

What a Gas!

Lavoisier thought there were 33 **elements**. Yet scientists soon found others. One of the first scientists to find new elements was Humphry Davy. He was an English chemist.

Davy first became known in 1799. He discovered a gas called nitrous oxide (also called laughing gas). He found that this gas could prevent people from feeling pain during operations.

Davy also discovered how to make powerful **batteries**. Early batteries were made from metal and chemicals. Davy used different metals and chemicals in his batteries. This made them more powerful.

Davy also showed how batteries made electricity. They made electricity because of **chemical reactions** inside them. A chemical reaction happens when chemicals join together or split apart. Chemical reactions make new **substances**. A substance is something that you can touch and see.

| battery | something that makes electricity using chemicals and metals |
| chemical reaction | when chemicals join together or split apart to make new substances |

◄ The first electric battery was invented in 1799 by Alessandro Volta.

Electric elements

Davy tried to split **compounds**. Compounds are **substances** made from two or more **elements**. At first Davy put the compounds in water. Then, he put electricity through the water. Yet the compounds did not split into elements.

Then, Davy tried **melting** the compounds. He heated them until they became liquids. Success! The compounds split. He found two new elements called sodium and potassium. Later, he found five more elements.

Davy discovered potassium. Potassium burns with a bright orange flame. ▲

Up to 1,000 people ▲
would come to see
Davy's talks.

Davy gave many talks about chemistry. People loved to watch his experiments. His talks were also very popular.

Chemists were at last beginning to understand elements. Yet they still didn't know very much about **atoms**.

21

Weighing Atoms

John Dalton was an English chemist. His ideas about **atoms** were different. He found that the atoms of different **elements** were different sizes. He even weighed them! Well, sort of . . .

Dalton figured out what each element weighed compared to hydrogen. He knew that hydrogen was the lightest element. He knew it had the lightest atoms. Dalton did not know the actual weight of a hydrogen atom. He just set the weight as 1.

Then, he figured out the weights of other atoms compared to hydrogen. Carbon is an element. Carbon has an **atomic weight** of 12. This means that an atom of carbon weighs twelve times more than an atom of hydrogen.

Billions of atoms

Today, scientists know the actual weights of atoms. They are pretty light! There are 50,000,000,000,000,000,000,000 (50,000 billion billion) atoms in 0.04 ounces (1 gram) of carbon.

atomic weight   weight of an atom compared to the weight of a hydrogen atom

◄ *Scientists can now see atoms using powerful microscopes. The different colors in this photo show different types of atoms.*

Dalton lived at about ▶ the same time as Humphry Davy.

The Amazing Chemist

Jons Berzelius was a teacher in Sweden. He lived at the same time as Humphry Davy and John Dalton. Berzelius discovered more **elements** than Davy. He also found that some of Dalton's **atomic weights** were wrong.

Berzelius also thought of a new way of writing the names of chemicals. He used symbols. The symbols used either one or two letters. They made writing the names of elements and **compounds** much easier.

Berzelius was ▶ really eager to teach chemistry. He made sure it was taught in schools!

How symbols can help

Chemical symbols can show what is in a compound. Water is a compound. Water is made of two atoms of hydrogen (symbol H). These are joined to one atom of oxygen (symbol O). Water can be written in chemical symbols as H_2O.

Symbols for some elements

H
hydrogen

C
carbon

O
oxygen

Ca
calcium

Na
sodium

Fe
iron

Au
gold

25

Making Sense of the Elements

Dmitri Mendeleev was a Russian chemist. He came up with a way to group the **elements**.

Mendeleev grouped the elements in order of their **atomic weight**. He discovered that every seventh element was similar. For example, element 2 (lithium) was similar to element 9 (sodium). Element 3 (beryllium) was like element 10 (magnesium). So, he organized the elements into a table of seven columns. He called it the **Periodic Table**.

Mendeleev was ▶ probably the hairiest chemist ever! When Russians were once asked to shave off their beards, Mendeleev refused!

The Periodic Table helped chemists to understand the elements. Below is is part of Mendeleev's original Periodic Table. The numbers are the atomic weights. Compare it with the modern Periodic Table on page 28.

Period	Group 1	Group 2	Group 3	Group 4	Group 5	Group 6	Group 7
1	**H** hydrogen 1						
2	**Li** lithium 7	**Be** beryllium 9.4	**B** boron 11	**C** carbon 12	**N** nitrogen 14	**O** oxygen 16	**F** fluorine 19
3	**Na** sodium 23	**Mg** magnesium 24	**Al** aluminium 27.3	**Si** silicon 28	**P** phosphorus 31	**S** sulfur 32	**Cl** chlorine 35.5
4	**K** potassium 39	**Ca** calcium 40	**–** [unknown] 44	**Ti** titanium 48	**V** vanadium 51	**Cr** chromium 52	**Mn** manganese 55
5	**(Cu)** copper 63	**Zn** zinc 65	**–** [unknown] 68	**–** [unknown] 72	**As** arsenic 75	**Se** selenium 78	**Br** bromine 80

Periodic Table   way of grouping the elements

The Periodic Table

The modern **Periodic Table** is a bit different from Mendeleev's. Many more elements have been discovered since Mendeleev created his table.

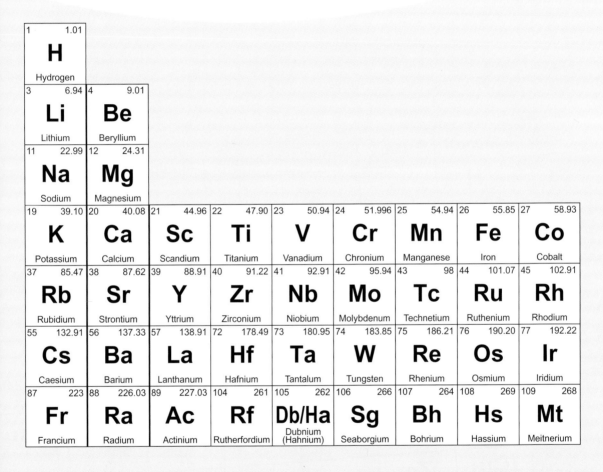

1 1.01 **H** Hydrogen								
3 6.94 **Li** Lithium	4 9.01 **Be** Beryllium							
11 22.99 **Na** Sodium	12 24.31 **Mg** Magnesium							
19 39.10 **K** Potassium	20 40.08 **Ca** Calcium	21 44.96 **Sc** Scandium	22 47.90 **Ti** Titanium	23 50.94 **V** Vanadium	24 51.996 **Cr** Chronium	25 54.94 **Mn** Manganese	26 55.85 **Fe** Iron	27 58.93 **Co** Cobalt
37 85.47 **Rb** Rubidium	38 87.62 **Sr** Strontium	39 88.91 **Y** Yttrium	40 91.22 **Zr** Zirconium	41 92.91 **Nb** Niobium	42 95.94 **Mo** Molybdenum	43 98 **Tc** Technetium	44 101.07 **Ru** Ruthenium	45 102.91 **Rh** Rhodium
55 132.91 **Cs** Caesium	56 137.33 **Ba** Barium	57 138.91 **La** Lanthanum	72 178.49 **Hf** Hafnium	73 180.95 **Ta** Tantalum	74 183.85 **W** Tungsten	75 186.21 **Re** Rhenium	76 190.20 **Os** Osmium	77 192.22 **Ir** Iridium
87 223 **Fr** Francium	88 226.03 **Ra** Radium	89 227.03 **Ac** Actinium	104 261 **Rf** Rutherfordium	105 262 **Db/Ha** Dubnium (Hahnium)	106 266 **Sg** Seaborgium	107 264 **Bh** Bohrium	108 269 **Hs** Hassium	109 268 **Mt** Meitnerium

58 140.12 **Ce** Cerium	59 140.91 **Pr** Praseodymium	60 144.24 **Nd** Neodynium	61 145 **Pm** Promethium	62 150.35 **Sm** Samarium	63 151.96 **Eu** Europium
90 232.04 **Th** Thorium	91 231.04 **Pa** Protactinium	92 238.03 **U** Uranium	93 237.05 **Np** Neptunium	94 244 **Pu** Plutonium	95 243 **Am** Americium

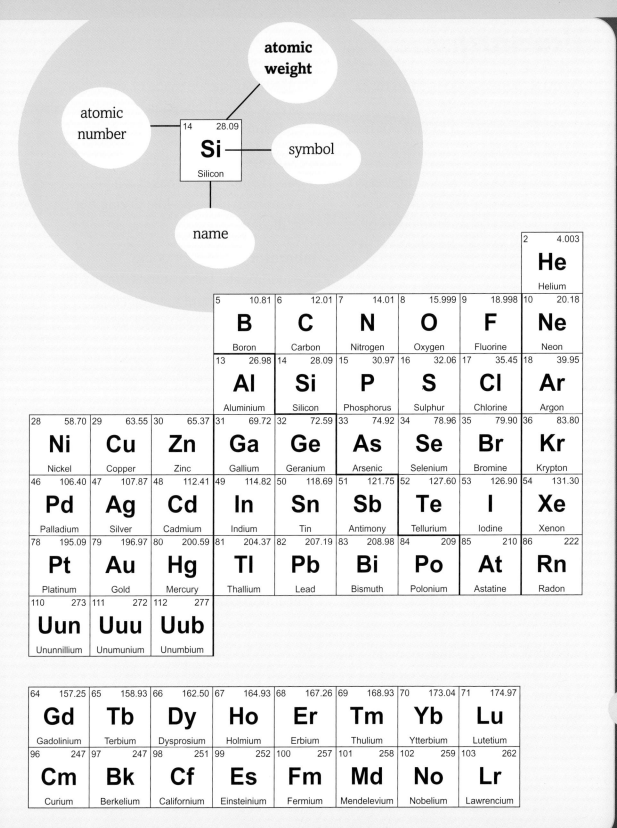

atomic number

atomic weight

symbol

name

14	28.09
Si	
Silicon	

2	4.003
He	
Helium	

5	10.81
B	
Boron	

6	12.01
C	
Carbon	

7	14.01
N	
Nitrogen	

8	15.999
O	
Oxygen	

9	18.998
F	
Fluorine	

10	20.18
Ne	
Neon	

13	26.98
Al	
Aluminium	

14	28.09
Si	
Silicon	

15	30.97
P	
Phosphorus	

16	32.06
S	
Sulphur	

17	35.45
Cl	
Chlorine	

18	39.95
Ar	
Argon	

28	58.70
Ni	
Nickel	

29	63.55
Cu	
Copper	

30	65.37
Zn	
Zinc	

31	69.72
Ga	
Gallium	

32	72.59
Ge	
Geranium	

33	74.92
As	
Arsenic	

34	78.96
Se	
Selenium	

35	79.90
Br	
Bromine	

36	83.80
Kr	
Krypton	

46	106.40
Pd	
Palladium	

47	107.87
Ag	
Silver	

48	112.41
Cd	
Cadmium	

49	114.82
In	
Indium	

50	118.69
Sn	
Tin	

51	121.75
Sb	
Antimony	

52	127.60
Te	
Tellurium	

53	126.90
I	
Iodine	

54	131.30
Xe	
Xenon	

78	195.09
Pt	
Platinum	

79	196.97
Au	
Gold	

80	200.59
Hg	
Mercury	

81	204.37
Tl	
Thallium	

82	207.19
Pb	
Lead	

83	208.98
Bi	
Bismuth	

84	209
Po	
Polonium	

85	210
At	
Astatine	

86	222
Rn	
Radon	

110	273
Uun	
Ununnillium	

111	272
Uuu	
Unumunium	

112	277
Uub	
Unumbium	

64	157.25
Gd	
Gadolinium	

65	158.93
Tb	
Terbium	

66	162.50
Dy	
Dysprosium	

67	164.93
Ho	
Holmium	

68	167.26
Er	
Erbium	

69	168.93
Tm	
Thulium	

70	173.04
Yb	
Ytterbium	

71	174.97
Lu	
Lutetium	

96	247
Cm	
Curium	

97	247
Bk	
Berkelium	

98	251
Cf	
Californium	

99	252
Es	
Einsteinium	

100	257
Fm	
Fermium	

101	258
Md	
Mendelevium	

102	259
No	
Nobelium	

103	262
Lr	
Lawrencium	

Glossary

alchemist person who tried to make gold from other substances. Alchemists also tried to find out how to live forever.

atom tiny piece that makes up every kind of substance. An atom is so small that you could fit millions of atoms into the period at the end of this sentence.

atomic weight weight of an atom compared to the weight of a hydrogen atom. Hydrogen has an atomic weight of 1 and carbon has an atomic weight of 12. This means that carbon atoms are twelve times heavier than hydrogen atoms.

battery something that makes electricity using chemicals and metals. Batteries are used to power many everyday objects.

chemical reaction when chemicals join together or split apart to make new substances. A chemical reaction happens when iron rusts.

compound chemical that is made of two or more elements joined together. Water is a compound made of the two elements, hydrogen and oxygen.

element substance made of only one kind of atom. Metals such as copper and aluminium are common elements.

evaporate turn from a liquid into a gas. Heating often makes a liquid evaporate, like a puddle drying out in the sun.

laboratory place for doing experiments. Laboratories are usually specially built and have scientific equipment for doing experiments.

melt turn from solid to liquid. Heating often makes a solid melt, like melting butter in a saucepan.

Periodic Table way of grouping the elements. The Periodic Table was created by Dmitri Mendeleev.

substance something that you can touch and see. Everything around you is made from substances.

urine mixture of water and unwanted chemicals from your body

Want to Know More?

Books

• Nardo, Don. *Atoms*. San Diego: Kidhaven, 2002.

• Oxlade, Chris. *Atoms*. Chicago: Heinemann Library, 2002.

• Oxlade, Chris. *Elements and Compounds*. Chicago: Heinemann Library, 2002.

Websites

• http://periodic.lanl.gov/ Check out this website to view the Periodic Table and to learn more about using the table. Sponsored by Los Alamos National Laboratory.

• http://education.jlab.org/index.html Would you like to learn more about atoms and elements? Visit this website to find out more and to play some games and puzzles! Sponsored by Jefferson Lab.

Find out about water, one of the simplest compounds, in *The Life and Times of a Drop of Water*.

Find out how different substances can be used to survive on a desert island in *A Matter of Survival*.

Index